Messages
to Self

A Practical Guide to Spirituality

JOAQUIN S. EVANS

This book is dedicated to you

Contents

MESSAGES TO SELF

Introduction

Why are you here? What are you looking for among these pages?

Whether we realize it or not, we spend much of our lives searching for things in the wrong places. As a result, those moments where we feel like everything is right with the world, those perfect days where we drift off to sleep at night with no worries on our mind, can be rare. This fact makes those moments precious to us, but what if I could help you increase the frequency of those perfect days? What if there was a way for you to have more perfect days than not from now on? What if the perfect day could become your norm? No, I'm not suggesting that there's some sort of magic trick that would ensure that all your days turn out exactly how you want them to. What I hope that I will be able to do for you is to help you see the world—and yourself—a bit differently, and; through a shift in your perspective, help you to create the type of life experience where having that perfect day will no longer be left up to chance or circumstance. I'm not going to spend a lot of time on this intro because I want to get right into helping you begin your journey towards becoming the best version of yourself that you could be. I just want you to know that you aren't alone in this. Life isn't easy, and we all must walk the Path as individuals, but at the same time, we are also a part of something much bigger than any single person. What I am about to say may sound strange for now, but it is truer than I can possibly explain to you in this short introduction.

I Am you, and you are me. We are each of us

what the other has the potential to become, and at the same time, we are much more than most people realize. We are all connected on a level so profound, yet so innate and simple, that it defies normal human perception and understanding. But, once we begin to remember who and what we really are we also begin to understand the truth of that connection in the depths of our being and our lives are forever changed.

The information I am going to offer you here isn't necessarily "new" information. Many Enlightened individuals have received the same knowledge throughout the centuries; similar teachings can be found in many religious texts and other divinely-inspired works. What I am here to offer you is a new perspective, one that makes the teachings accessible and understandable to a new group of people. I don't take credit for the knowledge itself; if anything I take credit for allowing myself to be used as the vessel/filter through which the knowledge once again flows into the world.

If you're ready to start the journey towards becoming the best version of yourself that you could possibly be, then I am ready to help you.

Let us begin.

Chapter One

What is your ultimate goal?

I wanted to start this journey off by asking this question because I feel as if knowing the answer (what I believe to be a fundamental truth), is necessary to approach becoming the best version of yourself from the right angle. This knowledge becomes the foundation for everything else we learn as we walk the Path and grow. Everyone I ask this question responds differently. The responses range from things along the lines of "to be the best parent to my children that I can possibly be," to things like "offering God my faithful service and love." But the truth is we all have the exact same Ultimate Goal—and that goal is to be happy. To enjoy our existence. Any other goals we come up with in life are either a product of running towards something that we believe will make us happy, or running away from something that we believe will make us uncomfortable (fear, sadness, pain, frustration etc.,) which is basically anything on the opposite end of the spectrum from happiness. Think about it like this, all of the goals you've ever set for yourself in life you chose because you believed that accomplishing them would bring you some level of happiness, even if it was the joy of seeing someone else happy. Otherwise, you wouldn't have chosen them as goals in the first place.

MISCONCEPTIONS

There are two common misconceptions that I

believe are the cause of the variation in answers:

1. The belief that attaining the goal is the goal itself, and

2. The belief that attaining the goal is the surest path to happiness (I believe that happiness is the goal, not the result).

These two misconceptions cause us to make what I believe to be two huge mistakes that put a more reliable and fulfilling type of happiness beyond our reach. We sacrifice our happiness in the moment for the possibility of attaining what we believe will bring us a bigger portion of it in the future, and we divide the happiness that we do have access to amongst many things—effectively leaving our happiness at the mercy of circumstance.

Here, let me explain.

You believe that suffering now will lead to success in the future, so you sacrifice today's happiness for tomorrow's reward. The problem with this way of thinking is you have no idea of how truly satisfied you'll be once you attain your goal, and, more importantly; none of us have been guaranteed that a tomorrow is in the plans for us. Because of our fear of the unknown, most of us avoid facing the very real possibility that we may run out of tomorrows before we ever reach the destinations we have in mind. Because we aren't guaranteed a tomorrow, the only thing that is truly real is this moment, the only thing that is certain in life is right now. This doesn't mean we should stop making plans for the future or working towards seeing them come to fruition; it simply means we should learn to enjoy our *now* as we chase our tomorrows. This can be accomplished through a shift in perspective rather than a change in circumstance.

Nothing in your life needs to improve for you to start enjoying it more—other than your way of looking at it. That's easy to say, but becoming capable of actually implementing it is the result of effort, openness, and honesty (especially in regard to our perception of self). We start to examine our motives, to confront our shortcomings and determine their deeper origins to rid ourselves of shame or misguided guilt. And we learn to make happiness a priority. It's a process, and it will take time, but it is definitely possible, and it is definitely worth it.

> Nothing in your life needs to improve for you to start enjoying it more—other than your way of looking at it.

HAPPINESS MISCONCEPTION

The other mistake many of us make is that we

take our happiness and divide it up amongst many things, then spend the rest of our lives trying to collect it from them. We become dependent on those things continuously being in good condition or working out how we want them to for us to feel satisfied with life. When I explain this concept, I tell people to think of their complete and perfect idea of happiness as a cookie (I know I know, lol.) What we do is we take that cookie and break it up into pieces, then we place a piece in the kind of car we drive, and another in the quality of clothes we wear. We place a piece in the type of job we have and a piece in the balance we have in our bank accounts. We place a piece in the status of our relationships, and the neighborhood we live in, and the size of the house we own. We place a piece in the type of life we can afford to provide for our children, and another piece in our appearance, and another in the food we eat, etc. The outcome of this practice is that we ensure that we will never be completely happy ever again (or at least rarely so.)

By doing this, we have divided our happiness up between a bunch of things that we ultimately have no control over, which means we have inadvertently left the possibility of having a good day up to chance.

Say you have the house you've always wanted in the neighborhood in which you want to raise your children, but then you get laid off from the dream job that was paying for it all. *happiness incomplete*

Say you have the house in the desired neighborhood and the dream job, but can't find the partner you wanted to share it all with. *happiness incomplete*

What if you were an attractive person with kids that adored you but you couldn't afford to give them the type of life you wanted them to have? *happiness incomplete*

Even if you had all the things you wanted in life that you believed would make you happy, it would only take one unfortunate event to ruin it for you in an instant. There's a better way, and I'm going to try to teach it to you. It won't remove the possibility of serious problems arising from time to time that have the potential to disrupt your happiness, but it *will* help to make sure that the small things that come up don't easily disrupt your happiness going forward. This will allow you to remain truly happy for longer periods of time. You'll also learn how to find your way back to happiness more quickly when unfortunate things do happen in your life that cause you to experience negative emotion.

The first thing we must learn to do is to become our own personal happiness generators. Instead of trying to find happiness in all of the things we discussed before, we learn to find happiness within *ourselves*, and then bring it with us into our interactions with those things and those people. One of the mantras I have come to live by is the phrase "I take my vibe wherever I go." Rather than depending on situations or things to create a feeling for me, I intentionally create it for myself through a shift in my perspective/consciousness, and then I carry it with me throughout the day. I accomplish this by way of some simple exercises and habits I have formed.

One of the practices I adopted was to actively begin to seek a perspective that either generates positive emotion or halts the production of negative emotion the moment that I encounter misfortune. I'm not talking about looking on the brighter side, more like looking at the bigger picture and being honest and objective about my circumstance. For example, if I bruised my shin, I might remind myself that the pain is temporary and is merely my body's way of helping me to protect myself. This practice isn't about pretending that your unfortunate circumstances are pleasant, it's about taking control of the narrative. In most cases, it's how we *think* about a situation more than the actual situation itself that determines how it affects us. Knowing this, we can consciously choose to look at things from a different angle to change how we experience them. Even practicing this technique I found that sometimes depending on the nature of the situation, I just wasn't able to shift my emotions from negative to positive and that's where this next technique comes in.

VISUALIZATION

The tool I found to supplement things was visualization exercises. I chose three things that I had a genuine desire to accomplish in my life, and I began to spend time each day visualizing those things in detail. I wouldn't just visualize them, I would go so deep into the exercise that it felt like I was actually living out these experiences. This would cause me to generate the same positive emotion that I would feel if I had actually attained these things already. In one of my early visualizations, I would picture myself standing on a beach with my eyes closed. I would feel the breeze coming off the water and blowing across my skin, and I would feel the sand between my toes with the sun shining on my back. I would feel my perfectly healthy body being filled with energy as I spent time in communion with and being acknowledged by God/The Universe. After spending some time perfecting these visualizations, I began to make use of them whenever I found myself in a situation where I was having a tough time producing positive emotion. I was now capable of closing my eyes for a few moments any time I wanted and creating a genuinely positive emotion for myself. Eventually what happens is you become so familiarized with the sensation of producing positive emotion that you can create it on demand without the need to make use of a visualization technique.

Imagine if instead of trying to find a car that would make you happy, you learned to generate a high level of happiness by your will alone. Then you could buy whatever car made sense financially and be just as satisfied with it as if you had bought your dream car. That doesn't mean that you stop working towards getting that dream car, it simply means that your happiness is no longer dependent on its acquisition. What we are discussing here is a concept called "attachment." An attachment could be described as an emotional dependence on something (remember that "cookie" analogy?). This may not sound like such a bad thing on the surface, but later on, we will discuss the "Law of Attraction," which describes how your thoughts and emotions draw positive and negative things into your experience. This means that giving something the power to shift your emotions could cause unforeseen, and potentially undesired results.

When trying to figure out the things you have an attachment to, ask yourself these questions:

1. Would not having access to that thing cause a recognizable shift in my mood?
2. Would a change in the quality of this thing cause a drastic shift in my emotional state?

I'm not talking about things we actually need like food, water, and shelter; I'm talking about things like alcohol, junk food, sex, and things like large amounts of money or expensive possessions. I must press this point home: there is nothing wrong with enjoying these things and wanting them to be present in our lives. The problems arise when they go from being a simple desire to a necessity in our eyes because this shift allows them to have a major impact on our mood and our actions. They don't necessarily need to be removed; we simply need to shift our perspective.

MOTIVE, MORALITY & EFFORT

One of the tools I use to accomplish this is an acronym I created, "M.M.E," which stands for "Motive, Morality, & Effort." In the beginning, I used this tool during moments of introspection to examine my actions in retrospect.

I would look at the actions I had taken in

any given situation, and I would ask myself three things:

1. What was the motive behind my actions? Was that motive pure?
2. Were my actions in line with my personal code of morality? and;
3. Did I put forth my best effort to accomplish what I set out to do?

Doing this in retrospect gave me some much-needed insight into my personal spiritual growth, but it also allowed me to remove my attachment to the outcome of situations while simultaneously freeing me from the practice of beating myself up over the mistakes I made. As long as I could look at myself and say honestly that my motive was pure, that I had conducted myself in a manner that upheld my personal code of morality, and that I had put forth my best effort, then I would be at peace with myself regardless of how things turned out.

I soon realized that I could also use this tool *preemptively* as well. Before I would commit to an action, I would run through the same checklist. This allowed me to dispel much of the fear associated with making big decisions and to avoid any self-recriminations or disapproval of my own conduct in hindsight. Before I would take action, I would ask, "Is my motive pure?" If my answer was "yes" then I would move on to the next question, if "no" then I wouldn't go through with the action. I would then ask myself "Is what I plan to do in line with my personal code of morality?" If it was not, then I wouldn't go any further but if it was, then all that was left to do was to commit to putting forth my best effort, and I could then move freely without the burden of worrying about the outcome. By using "M.M.E." in my daily life, I was able to avoid the anxiety and the fear of failure I had been accustomed to dealing with in the past and move that much closer to taking ownership of my experience.

> If we can learn to see the world, and ourselves differently, then we can begin to master taking control of our own happiness...

If we can learn to see the world, and ourselves differently, then we can begin to master taking control of our own happiness and begin to experience happiness on another level; one independent of the usual external influences. To accomplish this, we must gain a deeper understanding of our place in the world, our connection to all things, and our connection to our Higher Selves and God/The Universe/Mother Earth/Cosmic Consciousness (or whatever other aspect that resonates with us), which is ultimately the Source of all joy and happiness. The easiest way to gain a deeper understanding, and to begin to experience the joy that comes directly from the Source is to evolve/Ascend.

Ascension can be facilitated and ultimately

accomplished by working towards establishing a more seamless connection to our Higher Selves. The more seamless that connection becomes, the more insight we gain on all things by way of our intuitive gift; and the more we begin to see through the illusions set in place to challenge us. It isn't that the car or the house or the money isn't real, it's the nature and the significance of those things that is the illusion.

Another illusion we must learn to see through is the idea that the individual is separate from the whole, but don't worry too much about wrapping your mind around these concepts right now. In the near future, you won't have to figure things out on your own because you will have established a conscious connection to your Higher Self who will support you in your attempts to understand. This connection serves to provide a constant communion with God and therefore gives us access to all knowledge in existence. Instead of spending your time trying to acquire more and more knowledge, you'll spend your time and energy working on making the connection to your Higher Self more complete, and you'll find yourself beginning to just "know" things. Now is when we begin to work on developing your intuition.

Before we move on though, I need to make something clear: If you want to be successful at changing who you are, if you truly want to grow, don't make your motivation anything external.

Sure, thoughts of your children, significant other or God may influence the decision, but if you don't have a *personal* reason to pursue the change that takes precedence, then it will likely be a temporary thing. Without that personal reason, you would be attempting to make fundamental personal/internal changes while using an *external* source for motivation, which is usually a product of some sense of obligation or duty. My belief is that attempting to adhere to an adopted code of morality based on religion, or to an adopted ideal based on the influence of society, will not yield the most reliable results. Decide for yourself what your ideal idea of self is and work towards making that image a reality. Don't do it for God. Don't do it for your husband or wife or for your kids. Do it for yourself before anything else and understand that all the other people in your life will benefit from the decision as well by being granted access to a better version of you.

Chapter Two

Intuition

In the past, I thought of intuition as some sort of special psychic ability, but as I became increasingly familiar with it and began to use it in my day to day life, I realized that it wasn't some superpower that only a select few of us have. What I learned is that intuition is a gift that every single one of us is born with, one that requires maintenance to remain in good working order or it begins to atrophy and becomes unreliable. To reap the full benefits of our time here on this earth, and to prepare ourselves for what comes next, we must learn to make practical use of our intuition in our everyday lives. But there's a slight problem. With the current state that most people's sense of intuition is in, it is most likely extremely unreliable. So how do we build it back up? How do we strengthen it so we can begin to rely on it again like we were always meant to?

GUT DECISIONS

The best way to strengthen this ability is to use it! Start making decisions with your "gut" and then act on them so you can exercise it and begin to reestablish trust in it. But be aware, because you haven't been actively using it, there's a good chance that your intuition no longer functions properly. This means that until you strengthen your intuitive ability, it is going to steer you wrong much of the time. You're going to trust your gut on things, and it is going to lead you into circumstances and situations that you would have chosen to avoid if given the chance. The upside to this is that even the uncomfortable and unfortunate experiences are used by the Divine to facilitate our growth. Every decision we make is the right decision, for the simple fact that we have lessons to learn in every situation we find ourselves in whether pleasant or unpleasant. There are things to learn in both dark places and in the light, which is exactly how the system was designed to work.

MAKING USE OF INTUITION

I know the idea of your intuition leading you down difficult paths doesn't sound like much fun, but the point of beginning to make decisions based on your intuition isn't to make the "right" choices or even to reap the benefits of doing so immediately. The goal is *literally* just to start using it again so you can get it back in working order.

Let's say you broke your arm badly and couldn't use it for months. When you finally got the cast off would you immediately try to lift the heaviest amount of weight you had ever been capable of lifting? Of course not! You'd start rehabilitating it slowly over time with exercise. If you tried to lift something heavy with it and were unable to, would that cause you to give up on using your arm ever again? No way! Because you believe in your heart that it can be strong again if you just put in the work. Starting to actively use your intuition again isn't about being right or wrong, it's about muscle memory. Water rushing over rock doesn't immediately become the Grand Canyon, it carves a channel in the rock through repetition and persistence. At first that channel is shallow and unreliable, but the water persists, and slowly the channel deepens, and then more water begins to find its way into it causing the channel to widen and deepen at an even faster pace and then the rate of speed at which the water flows through it begins to increase and *now* things are really moving! The process becomes easier and more natural, it becomes automatic and smooth—that's when the *real* magic starts. That's when we start to be able to rely on that sense we had forgotten we had, the sense that this society never taught us to make proper use of. That's when our lives begin to become something more than they were before we began actively walking the Path once again. But first, we've got to make peace with the idea of using our intuition and being misled by it in the beginning.

Reactivating our gift of intuition can lead to us having a more beautiful experience in this plane of existence. It can help us in the decision-making process & send us down paths we would have never thought to take, leading us to discoveries that expand our minds and enhance our lives. Developing this gift becomes an absolute necessity in the next phase of our journey. I mentioned earlier that we needed to start practicing with our intuition now to prepare for what comes next. I said that because from what I understand, intuition is how we communicate and navigate in other planes of existence. Many of the times that I've had interactions with beings from other planes, our communication wasn't audible nor did it involve any gestures. I intuitively knew what they were trying to communicate to me and they in turn intuitively knew what I was trying to convey to them. No words were spoken out loud; there were no barriers created by language, I simply "knew" what they were saying and vice versa.

> "Intuition is how we communicate and navigate in other planes of existence."

COSMIC CONSCIOUSNESS

Think of earth and this plane of existence as an amazing training facility. We come here to learn the lessons we need to Ascend on the other side, and to enjoy ourselves. When I say that, I'm referring to my belief that there are different "levels" to dwell on when we cross over into other planes of existence. I believe gaining access to these other areas is dependent upon the level of Enlightenment we attain here in this plane of existence. There are lessons we can only learn while taking part in the Human Adventure, so we come back to this plane over and over while taking short rests on the other side until we have mastered them all. I believe that the final destination for us all is a return to constant conscious communion with God and harmonious inclusion in what I call the "All" or Cosmic Consciousness. I believe this return to be guaranteed for each of us, the only variable being how many incarnations it takes each soul to reach that point.

A monk once told me that the spiritual concepts and teachings that come easily to us are the lessons that we have already mastered in previous incarnations. In each new incarnation, when we experience our first true Awakening and begin to consciously walk the Path again, information and knowledge begin to find their way to us. As we come across each new piece to the puzzle our intuition allows the ideas to just "click." The knowledge resonates with us on an innate level; things seem so obvious that we can hardly believe that we were unable to comprehend these concepts before. Eventually, though, we inevitably run into something that *doesn't* come so easily to us. Don't be discouraged by this. It means that we have finally picked up where we left off in our last incarnation, and having a developed intuitive ability will make this next leg of the journey less difficult. *Now* is when the real work starts! Be mindful not to let your hardships hinder your effort. Don't be discouraged by your difficulties because this is also when we can begin to make real progress and conquer new territory. When you encounter these new trials, try to shift your perspective to one that produces feelings of excitement and not of discouragement. *Now* it's time to prove that this entire thing wasn't just some passing interest. Now it's time to put in the effort and energy to prove to your Self that you are committed to becoming the best version of *you* that you can possibly be. Your intuition will help guide you through learning these new lessons. You are being given the opportunity to overcome and to Ascend, be encouraged!

Chapter Three

Meditation

The Divine speaks to us constantly in whispers. Our connection to it is omnipresent, but the majority of the time we experience that connection as a very subtle sensation, so we tend to overlook it. We run into difficulty when attempting to perceive it mainly because our senses are constantly being inundated with information, and also because we assume that any interaction with God will be accompanied by an overwhelming sensation. This is not the case. Unless we make a conscious decision to go inward and to be still, all the information flooding our senses keeps us from picking up on the subtle omnipresent vibrations, and that's where the practice of meditation comes in.

In my opinion, we should first use meditation to seek out our Higher Selves, but before doing that we have to learn how to meditate "properly," and that's when the trouble starts, lol.

Almost all of us actively walking the Path eventually find our way to meditation, but many of us struggle with it at first. When are we supposed to do it and for how long? In what position? What do we actually *do* and what are we supposed to think about while we do it? What should we expect to see if we do it "right?" Now, this relaxing activity has turned into a task, and whether we want to admit it or not, it isn't fun lol. You try to mimic the posture you see in the pictures, but you can't get comfortable, and there's no possible way you can get your legs into that lotus position. Your back hurts from trying to sit up straight and even when you finally *do* manage to get semi-comfortable you can't clear your mind because you keep getting distracted by random songs and lines from movies. I get it! Now let's see if I can help you get a better grasp on things through some simple instructions and a shift in perspective.

POSTURE:

First, regarding posture, most Americans aren't used to sitting cross-legged. The people you see sitting that way comfortably have either grown up in a culture where sitting cross-legged is common or have trained themselves to be able to assume that position through a regiment of stretching. Don't beat yourself up if you can't immediately do it comfortably. In the United States, most of us grow up sitting in chairs, so Paramahansa Yogananda of the "Self-Realization Fellowship" suggests meditating in a straight-backed chair with feet flat on the floor and hands resting on the thighs with palms facing upwards.

Don't rest on the back of the chair, scoot forward, so you are sitting up straight under your own power, keeping your shoulders back and relaxed. This doesn't mean you should give up on learning to sit cross-legged because you won't always have a chair available to sit in, but you should work on getting that position down outside of your meditation time. When you are sitting down to meditate your entire focus should be on God/The Universe/Mother Earth/Cosmic Consciousness or whatever other aspect that resonates with you, as well as the specific concept you are contemplating for that session. Work on the technical aspect of sitting cross-legged some other time. What you are trying to accomplish physically during meditation is two-fold: relaxation and stillness. These two things are not the same.

You can absolutely be relaxed without being still, and you can be still without being relaxed, what we want is a combination of both. This can usually be accomplished by going through some method or process of relaxation first (breathing, tension exercises, etc.) and then, after accomplishing a relaxed state, focusing on your objective while attempting to remain as still as possible. Keep in mind that your overall health is going to have an impact on how effectively you can maintain proper posture and concentration. Does this mean that if you're out of shape that you can't meditate? Absolutely not, but it will be a lot harder to sit upright for an hour if you have a back problem, and much harder to focus if doing so involves ignoring a health issue that is begging for your attention. If you are unable to assume this position, consider some alternatives like laying on your back. The problem with this position is that most people have a harder time staying awake when they are laying down—but it is definitely possible if one is determined. Find a position that works for you and start your journey. Also, try not to force it. The journey is just as important as the destination, and being *willing* to put forth effort and to experience positive change in your life is the most important thing.

Don't beat yourself up when you run into difficulties and don't force yourself to continue if things aren't clicking for you at that moment. I personally believe the benefits of meditation to be cumulative so instead of sitting there uncomfortably for hours, work on it a little each day. Set a beginning goal to sit still for 5 minutes and then work your way up. If at the end of that 5 minutes you feel like you can keep going, then do so. If you aren't feeling it, stand up, pat yourself on the back for making a good effort, and come back to it another time.

SCHEDULE:

Regarding what times of day are most productive for meditation, early morning and nights work well because that's when most people are settling down and the world is less hectic—but what's most important is establishing a set schedule. I try to meditate at the same time every day as much as possible. This not only helps me avoid forgetting my daily session, but it also causes my body to anticipate my attempt to enter a meditative state, which makes the transition easier.

For me, sticking to a set schedule can be more difficult to accomplish in the evenings, but I find that my mornings are usually more uniform. I work mornings, so I get up an hour before the time I usually start getting ready for work, and I spend that hour in meditation. This gives me time for a quick stretch to loosen up my body before I sit down to relax into it. If I come out of the meditative state before the hour is up, I spend the rest of that time reading texts that revolve around spirituality. I also wake up early on my off days, so I don't break the habit that I have established, and I can always go back to sleep after meditation if need be but I usually don't feel the need to do so. Did you know that deep meditation offers some of the same benefits as deep sleep? I also try to get a session in before bed, preferably an hour before but if your schedule just won't allow it, then when you head off to bed lay down and meditate yourself to sleep.

> Did you know that deep meditation offers some of the same benefits as deep sleep?

The goal should be to carry the peace from your morning meditation with you throughout the day and then to renew that peace before you head off to bed. Let your first and your last thoughts be focused on your search for the Divine and your pursuit of becoming the best version of yourself that you can possibly be. My *favorite* time to meditate is actually in the middle of the day. I find that I can be much more productive and go much deeper when I am entering a meditative state while well rested and fully awake.

The trick to not skipping out on days and really making a commitment is reminding yourself of the importance of what you are trying to accomplish. You aren't doing this for any superficial reasons, you're trying to make contact with God/The Divine and to evolve as a person. You're trying to establish a

You're trying to establish a stronger connection to your Higher Self and create a more enjoyable life experience.

stronger connection to your Higher Self and create a more enjoyable life experience. There is nothing more important. Accomplishing this will improve every other aspect of your life.

FOCUS:

The purpose of meditation, *true* meditation, isn't relaxation. The true purpose of meditation is communion with God/The Divine. You've probably been focused on trying to see some sort of visions or signs, colorful clouds or the *All-Seeing Eye* or whatever else you've read that other people have seen lol. I know, I was looking for the same things in the beginning myself. By making relaxation or seeing visions our objective rather than seeking God or Enlightenment, we only hinder our progress and cause ourselves to become frustrated when we don't see or feel what's expected. I was told that if what we see is darkness when we close our eyes to meditate, then we should assume that is exactly what God wanted us to see at that time and that there is a purpose behind the experience. That way of thinking led to a shift in my own perspective that has paid off, and I would later come to realize I was being taught a lesson on attachments.

I stopped thinking of meditation as some task I had to complete to Ascend and reminded myself that I was supposed to be coming out of it happy and rested, not tired and frustrated. In the beginning, I always went into my meditations with the intention of receiving something, but as I progressed I began to realize that I also had something to give. I stopped looking at it as merely a training session and started seeing it as my opportunity to offer God my time, my stillness, and my attention. As I make my offering, I feel love and peace being offered to me in return, flowing down into and through me as it refreshes and heals me. I let it root me, holding me steady in its embrace, and I can make space for more of my Higher Self to take up residence within this vessel.

Have you ever had a child give you his or her last piece of candy?

The innocence of the act touches your heart; it makes you want to buy that kid a *truckload* of candy, right? Lol, try this, the next time you sit down to meditate, imagine out of all the happiness that exists in the universe that you have a little piece for yourself. Whatever the amount is it doesn't matter. You may have had a bad day today and feel like you can only pull together a single drop of happiness to give, but when you sit down to meditate, I want you to offer that drop of happiness to God/The Universe—the same way that child offered you their last piece of candy. Offer it with your *entire being*. Feel that small amount of happiness and get to know it intimately and personally. Recognize that it isn't much, but it's all you have. Then freely offer it to God with love, adoration, and selflessness. In the back of your mind believe that He/She/It is going to feel the same way you felt when that child offered you their last and will want to *infinitely* multiply what you have offered them, showering you with happiness, love, adoration, and affection in return. Anything we offer freely to God is multiplied without fail.

I don't meditate in the same manner or focus on the same objective every time I have a session. Sometimes I go into a session with the sole intent to offer my love and gratitude to the Infinite. Sometimes I go into it with the intent to focus on a specific concept - like my connection to all things in existence, or to ponder the nature of my being. Ultimately, the two underlying themes that are ever-present in my meditations are gratitude, understanding/realizing who and what I Am, and becoming more cognizant/taking a more active role in my omnipresent connection to God.

THOUGHTS

The other part of this process is learning how to deal with all the unwanted thoughts and images that pop into your head. Eventually you'll reach a point where you won't have to deal with them at all, but initially, you may need to use some sort of method. When that song pops into your head, and you notice your inner voice singing the lyrics just stop singing and mentally say the word "Release," then let the thoughts dissipate as you refocus on your objective. Gently gaze outward and slightly upward and imagine yourself seeing by way of your third eye rather than the two you normally see with. Allow your vision to move in and out of focus as it wills but try to keep your eyes themselves still and focused on a solitary point. No straining or forcing it! Lol! Try not to project annoyance or frustration over the random things popping into your mind because this will only distract you more. Many people waste time and energy on the fruitless effort of trying to "stop" their thoughts or clear their mind indefinitely. The truth is we cannot halt the movements of our thoughts, but we *can* sink deep enough into meditation that they become background noise. Eventually, you reach a level where they no longer receive any of your attention.

A shift in perspective that makes this easier to accomplish is deciding to no longer see those thoughts as part of our self-image. Author Michael Singer often speaks about the nature of

We are not the thoughts themselves nor are they reflections of who we are.

a subject/object relationship. He says we, the beings, are the *subjects* and our thoughts are the *objects*. We are not the thoughts themselves nor are they reflections of who we are. We are the awareness that *observes* those thoughts. The Mind is a tool, and when we aren't actively using it to accomplish some task like solving a math problem, it doesn't shut off. No, it simply begins to produce "random" thoughts and you can't stop it from doing so no matter how hard you try but the reality is you really don't need to! For the purposes of meditation, you don't need to stop the thoughts from being generated, you merely need to shift your attention away from them. When you're sitting in your living room with the TV on and you're focused on the conversation you're having with a friend, you completely lose track of what is happening on the television. You didn't turn the TV off, you just shifted your attention so thoroughly that what was happening on that TV screen lost all meaning and importance. This perspective can also be applied to our day to day lives outside of meditation. Once you separate your idea of self from your thoughts, and you realize that you can consciously decide when or when not to pay attention to them, you've taken a huge step towards learning to achieve a consistent state of peace. As you implement this same practice during meditation you will find yourself able to go deeper into the meditative state and some things other than thoughts may begin to present themselves to you. This is normal. If visions come, cool, if clouds of color and light come, cool, but they aren't your goal. Finding God is your purpose so if those things don't happen for you immediately don't worry, stay with it.

A lot of people get to this stage and become distracted by the sights which can cause them to take much longer to Ascend. At first, it's hard for them to sit still, but gradually they start making progress. Then they start seeing occasional colors and lights and those lights start to show up more and more often, until one day they begin to see actual *visions*. As soon as they start to see visions, they become fixated on seeing them and never graduate to the next level. If all you see is darkness for the next six weeks, I want you to assume you are growing regardless of what it looks like on the surface and be thankful. The Path to Enlightenment and to the Divine is paved in gratitude

What most people disregard is the fact that God *wants* us to pursue Him/Her/It/Them, and God also wants us to become the best versions of ourselves that we can be. The same way Jesus came to remind us that the Sabbath was made for us, I'm here to remind you that meditation and the Path itself were made for us as well. Stop looking at your journey as a task and start seeing it as an adventure. Stop seeing your meditation as a chore and start seeing it as an opportunity, an offering to God, an activity that was meant to both relax and rejuvenate us. Start seeing your meditation as a tool by which we can save ourselves from our circumstance, and find our way to growth and everlasting freedom. Remember that meditation is an activity we were meant to enjoy, and that Meditation leads to Acceleration.

Chapter Four

Acceleration

Most people find themselves on the Path after having an Awakening. That initial Awakening usually isn't a result of any conscious effort to become Enlightened; it's usually just the moment God chooses for us to "wake up" and begin consciously walking the Path again. After we've had our first Awakening, we must begin putting in conscious effort to facilitate our Ascension. This effort usually comes in the form of reading, fellowshipping with others, and meditation and contemplation. Consistent meditation with the proper focus leads to accelerated Ascension, but what *is* Ascension exactly?

The concept of Awakening could accurately be described as becoming self-aware. My definition of *Ascension* is an expansion of one's consciousness by establishing a more seamless connection to one's Higher Self. This expansion is, in fact, a return to our truest form, our most natural state. The best way I can illustrate this process is to give you a bit more insight into the nature of our existence, while also providing you with an analogy and some clear imagery.

Ascension = an expansion of one's consciousness through establishing a more seamless connection to one's Higher Self.

My first true moment of Enlightenment/Self Realization in this incarnation was the moment I received the Truth that my Higher Self and my human self are the same being/entity. What I believe is that the Higher Self dwells in another plane of existence but can send a piece of itself (my human consciousness) into this plane of existence to occupy a human body and take part in what I call the "Human Adventure." The purpose of this process is to learn lessons that can only be learned here in this plane. The Higher Self never truly loses contact with that piece of itself, but the perception of that connection can be difficult from this end until we have made some progress on the Path. Because of this arrangement, Ascension basically involves "downloading" more of our Higher Self into this human vessel. Though the idea of separation is an illusion (we'll discuss this concept later), I want you to imagine your human consciousness as a cup of water with black dye in it. Imagine your Higher Self/Consciousness as a gallon of pure water. What we want to do is mix the pure water with the dyed water, but first, we've got to create enough space to accommodate the new volume of water we wish to bring in. In the case of the human body, we would need to "expand" both consciously and spiritually to make room for more of our Higher Consciousness. But, for the sake of the analogy, let's pretend that we merely purchased a larger container and poured the cup of dyed water into it in preparation. Now that we're prepared to receive more, imagine pouring the pure water slowly into the container with the cup of dyed water. As the container begins to fill and the pure and dyed waters mix, the cup of dyed water doesn't cease to exist, it merely becomes a part of something bigger than itself. The pure water becomes the more visible of the two but the dye is still in there whether we're able to see it or not. The more pure water that is poured into the vessel, the faster our Ascension occurs.

I believe that Ascension occurs in three phases: Preparation, Acceleration, and Manifestation. We'll discuss the Manifestation phase later.

> Ascension occurs in three phases: Preparation, Acceleration, and Manifestation.

PREPARATION

During the Preparation phase, Ascension seems almost effortless. You're discovering new things, and your consciousness is expanding quickly, but gently. Your intuition is awakening once again, you're connecting with like-minded individuals, and you're having the time of your life! It feels like you've discovered your destiny and have begun operating within your purpose as if God/The Universe/Mother Earth/Cosmic Consciousness is cradling you and carrying you to the place you were always meant to be. Absolutely everything is right with the world until suddenly it isn't anymore lol. Welcome to the Acceleration phase, which in my opinion is the scariest of the three.

ACCELERATION

When you begin to accelerate, everything that was weighing you down—like counterproductive ways of thinking, habits that have been impeding your progress, and attachments to things - will all begin to fall away. People in your life who don't match your speed or compliment your Walk will fall away as well. Not because they are unworthy or anything of that nature, they are simply in a different phase at the moment, and their Path is moving in a different direction. If you don't understand why this is happening, this part of the process can be tough. Sometimes it manifests as an inexplicable shift in your personal desires regarding your life. You become restless, no longer satisfied with the current state of things and you begin to experience an overwhelming urge to pursue something greater. Other times it can be a bit more uncomfortable. You lose that job you've had for years, your partner starts acting out of character forcing you to end things, or they end the relationship themselves, that dish you love to eat at that one restaurant makes you sick and now you don't want it anymore. Your best friend betrays you, that car you love gets totaled, your bank account takes a major hit, and you have a serious health scare. You're starting to feel like the world is coming down on you and God must be mad at you, or that you must have done something wrong to deserve this. What I want you to do right now is *be still*. You aren't being punished, you are being purified and positioned to receive. Without realizing what's happening, you may find yourself fighting the process and multiplying your suffering.

During this phase, a lot of the negative karma you have built up over time will be cleared. This could be the karma from a single lifetime, or many, many lifetimes—depending on your trajectory and what's waiting for you in the next leg of your journey. The process for clearing negative karma always includes some discomfort, but most people increase their discomfort exponentially because they won't let go and surrender to the process. They try to hold on to all the things that God is removing from their lives because they haven't realized that what's happening to them is in response to some of the things they have been asking God for. When you asked God for whatever it was—your prayer was sincere, it came from a place that most aren't truly familiar with, it was a request made by your Higher/Truer Self and Father/Mother/The Universe instantly honored it and began preparing you to receive but the process won't always be pleasant. Also, due to our limited foresight, it usually doesn't appear as if we are being led in a direction that will result in us getting that thing we want. Because we can't see it, we don't go with the flow, and we don't put forth our best effort even when we do. By allowing the Universe to order our steps, not only do we have a much greater chance of acquiring what we want, but it is very likely that we'll be guided to things that we never even imagined and we will enjoy those things even *more*. The Preparation phase is actually a lot of fun. Everything seems to fall into place perfectly and it feels like you're winning without even trying! Because of this, the Acceleration phase can seem like a nightmare in comparison if you aren't connected enough to see the "why" of it as it is happening, and even then, it still remains a trial for us all.

BENEFITS OF ACCELERATION

One of the major benefits of the Acceleration phase is that it exposes the areas in our lives and in ourselves that need improvement. In the Preparation phase, we can fall into the habit of assuming we are further along on the Path than we truly are because of the ease with which we assimilate things. The Acceleration phase gives us a clear picture of exactly how far we have come and how far we still have to go. It shows us very specific areas we need to focus on, lessons we need to learn, and short-comings we need to deal with and overcome. It sort of feels like being placed in a "sink or swim" scenario where our weaknesses begin to show themselves and the Force that has been supporting us since we first had our Awakening may feel as if it has been reduced, or even like God has become more distant. You may feel as if you have lost your way, but I want you to have faith in your Self and remain focused during this phase of the journey. You aren't lost, this is just the part of learning how to ride a bike where your parent takes their hands off the bicycle to see if you're ready to take full control of it yourself. Since your Awakening, you've been acquiring knowledge and new skills and evolving at a fast pace. Now you're being provided an opportunity to become familiar with your own strength, and to put the philosophical things you've been learning to practical use. The Acceleration phase is a period of tough love.

My personal experience with the process of Acceleration involved becoming extremely ill after having been completely healthy for 12 years prior. The doctors did all the tests imaginable and couldn't figure out the source of my problems. Throughout the ordeal, I was receiving messages from my Higher Self that told me that this was happening in response to the requests I had made to God. I was being told that it was now time for me to begin learning how to Create, how to consciously and intentionally manifest the things I wanted—including a healthy body—and to draw away from relying on illusions to sustain me. Everything God gives us is multi-purposed, even the pain He/She/It allows us to experience. The discomfort my body was being put through was part of the process of clearing my karma, but it was also being used to encourage me to learn how to take control of my experience in this plane of existence.

Up until that point, I had simply been asking God for things and leaving it up to Him/Her/It to bring those things to fruition. Now I was being challenged to create the things I wanted for myself through the power and authority I had been born with but had been ignorant of for much of my life. The power that was mine by birthright as a child of Divinity. No longer would everything be handed to me, now I would either learn to make use of my gifts, or I would be returning for another incarnation. It wasn't so much about gaining any new power or ability, it was about remembering what I was and realizing the power that my status as I Am (part of the All that is) granted me, and beginning to utilize it consciously.

> I was being challenged to create the things I wanted for myself through the power and authority I had been born with...

The Acceleration phase is when I became more aware of my omnipresent connection to God by way of my connection to my Higher Self. This is when I truly began to understand that separation is an illusion and that my Higher Self isn't simply some separate being whom I could call upon when in need. This was when I realized that I Am my Higher Self and that what I called intuition was simply my Self speaking to me and giving me guidance. I was the source of my intuition, and I had all the knowledge in existence at my disposal if I could learn to access it. Now I needed to learn the art of Manifestation.

Chapter Five

Manifestation

The concept of "I Am" isn't something that can be explained to you, it's something a person can only truly understand once they have experienced it personally. Everything and everyone in existence are connected via an omnipresent connection to God/The Universe/Cosmic Consciousness. The statement "I Am" reflects the realization of this, a declaration of one's understanding of their identity as an individual, indivisible part of the whole (the human race, the Universe, God, Energy, *everything*). This means that when looking at life from the perspective of the bigger picture, it is impossible for me to lack anything in truth because I have every single thing that anyone in existence currently has or has ever had. That may sound a bit outlandish on the surface,

> I have every single thing that anyone in existence currently has or has ever had.

but once you've consciously experienced the "I Am" state, I think my meaning will become more clear to you. Let's think of it this way: Would you say that your right hand is yours? In other words, do you own it? It is definitely a part of your body, but it also has an individual identity. Your right hand is not the same as your left foot, is it? It is unique even when compared to something similar like your left hand, but it is still a part of the whole that is you. Would your left hand ever become jealous of your right hand, or covet something that was held in it? Of course not, because both of your hands are a part

74

of you, so by default anything that one has the other has as well. You don't feel any sense of lack because you aren't holding something in both hands. You understand that regardless of which hand the object is in, it is ultimately in your possession. The inverse is true as well. If you own something, so does your right hand due to its inclusion as part of the whole being/entity that is you.

When I had reached a certain stage in my Walk, I began to think this way about all things in existence. If I own something, then it is yours, and if you own something, then it is mine as well. If it is in your hand, then it does not necessarily have to be in mine because your hand *is* my hand. There is no power or possession that I do not already have. There is nothing that exists whether ability, object, or information that I do not have access to. If it has been obtained by anyone, then I have obtained it as well. If it has been done, then I have done it. If it is possible, then I can do it. This doesn't mean that I no longer have the desire to achieve personal goals or to acquire things as an individual, it simply means that I no longer feel any pressure to do so or experience any anxiety in regard to my personal pursuits. This gives me the freedom to create goals for myself based on what my heart truly desires without the limitations placed on my imagination by thoughts of what my human mind believes to be reasonable or logical. Reaching this point on the Path allows you to pursue any goal without fear of failure. With that block removed, we begin to go further, reach higher and make bolder choices that lead to us seeing corresponding results. This state of existence is exactly what lead me to write this book, something I had been talking about doing for years but had always put off because of one excuse or another.

I started this chapter off with a discussion on the concept of "I Am", because most of what I come across regarding manifestation focuses on the practical application of it for the purpose of acquiring things. I'll touch on this as well, but I feel it's important for you to understand that manifesting things in this plane of existence isn't the sole purpose of our given ability. Just like intuition, we make use of manifestation on the other side, and both of these abilities are used in conjunction with one another. We learn to use our intuitive ability first because it facilitates our learning of other abilities, such as manifestation. Intuition is also how we know what to manifest in the first place.

MOVEMENT AND FORM

The two specific areas in which I believe the power of manifestation will play a key role are movement and form. Regarding movement, I believe our ability to manifest will be what makes traveling possible in the next plane of existence. I don't believe we will walk from point A to point B on the other side; I believe we will simply "will" ourselves to manifest wherever we would like to go be it 20 feet away or 20 miles. Regarding form, I believe our power of manifestation is how we will create things on the other side, and I also believe it is what we will use to create and maintain the forms we choose for ourselves. In our Truest form, I believe we are all beings made entirely of energy/light so we will have to manifest/create whatever other form we wish to take and hold that form using will power once we shed our human bodies and cross over. We develop abilities like intuition and manifestation here on earth so that we can practice using them and increase our proficiency with the process.

> We develop abilities like intuition and manifestation here on earth so that we can practice using them and increase our proficiency with the process.

78

THE THREE UNIVERSAL LAWS

To begin learning how to physically manifest things, you should first become familiar with three universal laws introduced to the world most recently by a woman named Esther Hicks, who channeled a group of beings who call themselves "Abraham" and received these teachings.

The three laws are:

- The Law of Attraction
- The Law of Deliberate Creation, and
- The Law of Allowing

The Law of Attraction basically says that you attract things in relation to your emotions (because your emotion produces vibrational resonance), and your emotion is a product of how you think. Positive or negative, good or bad, you will attract things into your experience that perpetuate whatever emotion you are producing (specifically that which you think about most), and it will happen whether you intend it to or not.

79

The Law of Deliberate Creation states that you can use your knowledge of the Law of Attraction to deliberately draw *specific* things into your life by focusing on them, and intentionally causing yourself to feel the emotion that having them would produce. This includes things like cars and money but also includes situations and circumstances. For example, getting closer to God or establishing a deeper connection to your Inner Voice or Higher Self.

Lastly, the idea of the Law of Allowing is learning to allow others to be exactly what they want and who they are without creating any emotional attachment to your assessment of their choices, or at the least not allowing yourself to dwell on your negative sentiments in regard to them. Actively disapproving of someone else's choices in life, even if only internally, will shift your emotion negatively and attract things and situations into your experience that do the same. In other words, you may attract things and situations that you will not enjoy. The idea is not to pretend as if you like the things you don't like or to force yourself to like them; the idea is to not *focus* on them. When you catch yourself thinking about something you dislike and experiencing the emotion that you do not enjoy, consciously shift your thoughts to something that you *do* enjoy so that your mood and thus the vibrations you are producing shift along with it. You will then begin to draw into your existence things and experiences that you will enjoy.

This isn't about being fake, it's about taking control of your emotional state and learning to harness your creative gift by intentionally choosing what to think about and what to focus on. If you think too long about what you *don't* want to happen, then by default you soak in the negative emotion that those thoughts generate and produce corresponding vibrations. This means you are in fact attracting those very things into your experience. The Law is simple, you attract that which you think most about and feel the strongest emotions over.

THE ORIGIN OF JOY

The other secret is that joy finds its origins in God/The Universe. Everything you can think of that would make you happy was created by God directly or indirectly. For example, God made the man that made the Ferrari. You can use the Laws to acquire a Ferrari and you *will* get it and it *will* make you happy for a time, but not nearly as happy as you could possibly be. If you finally achieved a conscious, direct connection to God/The Universe/Cosmic Consciousness or whatever you want to call it, then the bliss you would feel, and the peace and joy you would experience would make all other things seem trivial in comparison.

In my opinion, the smart thing to do would be to use the Laws to attract that which will help you establish a stronger connection to God, thus giving you access to the highest possible level of happiness, and inadvertently attracting other things into your life that are related to your personal idea of happiness. It all comes back to becoming skilled at consciously shifting your own perspective to produce the desired results.

THE NATURE OF THE PROCESS

Another thing I want to touch on regarding the concept of manifestation is the nature of the process. When I first began to consciously walk the Path, I would simply petition the Universe to attain the things I desired, and the Universe would respond and provide. But as I progressed, I began to notice a change in the way things were working. Where before I could simply petition the Universe and my Higher Self and then wait patiently to receive what I had asked for, I suddenly noticed that the response to these requests began to come in the form of Divine inspiration rather than being presented with the object of my desire. The message I was receiving was that my Higher Self would no longer simply work *for* me but would often begin to work *through* me or *with* me. In other words, I had been given enough wisdom to begin to consciously create the experience I desired for myself.

From this point on anything that I wanted for myself would require personal action on my own behalf. Prayer and meditation would now simply allow me to present my desires to my Higher Self and in turn allow the Universe to point me in the right direction and provide me with guidance as to how I could acquire these things myself. Most people think of manifestation as the ability to literally create something where there once was nothing, or the ability to magnetically attract that which we want to ourselves. But there is another facet to manifestation, one where we use meditation and visualization to make our heartfelt desires known to our Higher Selves, and then through intuition we receive guidance that presents us with the keys to obtaining them. I want to be clear about something here however. Most human beings don't know themselves well enough to make an educated decision in regard to choosing what they want for themselves. What I've found to be true in my own case is that God/The Universe/Cosmic Consciousness knows me much better than I know myself, and when I allow that Force to guide my steps I find myself enjoying life more than I could have imagined previously. Don't be afraid to move your feet when your intuition is leading you in a direction you don't think makes sense at the time. Mastering the art of manifestation is when we truly begin the transition from an existence as honest beggars to becoming the authors of our own experience.

Conclusion

This is just the beginning. The purpose of this book was to be somewhat of a catalyst. As I was writing it, I never thought of it as holding the answers to anyone's questions. I see it as simply another step on the Path for those seeking Enlightenment, for those who feel deep down that there is more happiness to be had in this life. This book is for those chasing God, and for all those beautiful Souls out there working towards becoming the best versions of themselves that they could possibly be.

I wrote this for the people who need it. My hope more than anything is that it ignites a spark within you that causes you to seek out Truths for yourself, and prompts you to begin to establish a tangible connection of your own to Cosmic Consciousness/The Universe. What I hope you found hidden in the pages of this book isn't just knowledge, I hope you found inspiration. I've not come to divulge all the secrets of the Universe to you, I've been sent to facilitate your thinking. You have access to all the same information and knowledge that I have access to, because you each have your own personal connection to the Source. Don't worry about trying to memorize information. What's important is establishing a stronger connection to your Higher Self, and that will happen naturally as your perspective begins to change and your consciousness begins to expand.

Remember, God doesn't expect perfection from us, He/She/It only expects effort. Go with God, become the light you've been searching for, and free the Minds.

#MessagesToSelf

Practice

Advice and Things to Contemplate

I left this section separate from the rest of the book because there is a particular way I wanted people to approach reading it. I am asking readers to read through it one concept at a time. After you have read through a single concept, do not proceed immediately to the next. I want you to spend some time in thought about the idea presented to you. This does not mean that you should agree with the concept, the purpose of this section is to give direction to your thoughts and to facilitate deeper thinking not necessarily to inform. After you have spent time in contemplation on one concept, whether a day or a week, then move on to the next concept and repeat the process. And remember, this is an adventure, not a race. Have fun!

"Less learning and more reflecting, that is how you will transition and transcend."

Very often what I see from those who have experienced an Awakening is a mad scramble to amass as much knowledge on the subject of Awakening/Enlightenment/Truth as they possibly can. That might sound like a good idea but it's actually the reason I believe so many people end up feeling like they're stuck in one place, like they've stopped making progress and are now simply chasing that feeling from when they first became conscious of the Path once again. What happens when we experience an Awakening is our eyes are opened to a whole new world of information and way of thinking. It's all so exciting and new, but because of this we tend to lose sight of the *purpose* for our Awakening and become fixated on collecting what I like to call new "Jeopardy facts." Our journey down the Path becomes a game where we collect Truths like shiny new objects to show off to our peers. We begin to secretly take pride in our spiritual Awakening, we become addicted to the sensation we get from each new revelation, and we begin to chase that "ah ha!" moment. The moment our focus changes from chasing God/creating a better version of ourselves to chasing knowledge, our progress slows down drastically. You've had an Awakening, you've discovered things about yourself and about the world that you never imagined, but don't settle for surface knowledge.

The only way to truly internalize the knowledge is to spend time in contemplation of it, to personalize it with your own perspective and to put it to good use. There is much more out there for you to know, but you probably won't find it in a book. The books are meant to help you start to think, to give you some guidance and direction, but no one can explain to you what "I Am" truly means or what Self Realization *feels* like. I can tell you a hundred different ways what I found out when I received the Gift, and you still won't fully understand until it is finally given to you. Then *you* won't be able to explain it either lol. It's not enough to just read about someone else's experiences, you've got to have them for yourself to truly understand. Reading is a good thing, but make sure you spend just as much if not more time in contemplation/meditation on the things you have read.

Reflections:

MESSAGES TO SELF

"The answers one receives are a direct reflection of the questions one asks. To learn more profound Truths, one should spend time deciding on more profound questions to ask..."

Reflections:

"Awakening is a process not a distinction or a destination."

Many think of Awakening regarding a person either being Awake or not, but it isn't that simple. Awakening/Enlightenment/Self Realization is a process, one in which we experience a series of Awakenings not a single event. Most people who claim to be "awake" have merely had their first Awakening in their current incarnation, one that is meant to cause them to begin consciously walking the Path to Enlightenment/Self Realization once again. For many, this will be the beginning of the end because instead of this becoming the launching point for their pursuit of Enlightenment, they believe themselves to have arrived at their destination, and so they stop seeking Ascension. They believe themselves to have been Awakened, so they cease pursuing their Awakenings, but in reality, they have merely fallen victim to pride. Even once you've Ascended to a level where further incarnations in this plane of existence are no longer necessary, there are *still* lessons to be learned in the next, a whole new plane of existence to explore and new heights to reach. Don't let your successes be your downfall, keep going!

Reflections:

MESSAGES TO SELF

"That which will exist, does exist..."

The human idea of separation is a falsehood, an illusion, a misunderstanding, a lie by omission. This misunderstanding has led us to think of time as linear, but in truth, our past, our present, and our future are all happening simultaneously. Think of life as an infinite moment. If you are *going* to have it, realize that you *already* have it. Begin to think of it in terms of it already being yours, and so shall it be.

Reflections:

....

_____

....

_____

....

_____

MESSAGES TO SELF

"First we learn to create a happier more fulfilling life, then we learn to escape it..."

Do not become confused about what the objective is during your pursuit of Enlightenment. You will absolutely improve the quality of your life/experience in this plane of existence by pursuing Enlightenment/Self-Realization, but that should not be mistaken as the goal, it is simply a wonderful side effect of consciously walking the Path. The goal is to once again become active participants in our connection to the Divine. By working to become conscious of the nature of our existence while still occupying our earthly forms, we can Ascend to a point where we escape the cycle of reincarnation and can begin the next leg of our journey. There are plenty of pleasurable experiences to be found in this plane of existence, but this is only the beginning.

MESSAGES TO SELF

Reflections:

*"You are living today in the experience that was
created by the choices you made yesterday."*

Reflections:

"Remember who you were before the troubles of the world taught you to be someone else. That is who you were meant to be..."

In the beginning of each new incarnation, I believe we are the closest to the level of Enlightenment we attained in our previous incarnations. As we grow, the illusions of the world begin to impose themselves on us. This influence is reinforced by the other Travelers we come in contact with who themselves have become thoroughly engrossed in those same illusions. Ascension involves a return to a childlike state. Not in the sense that one should become naive, but in the sense that one's outlook on life becomes much more simplified. Mastery = Simplicity.

Reflections:

"When we change ourselves we change the world, when we change the world we change ourselves..."

One day you will understand that separation is truly an illusion, and that there is no difference between the inside of myself and outside of myself.

Reflections:

_____

_____

_____

_____

_____

_____

_____

_____

"The Path to Enlightenment is paved in gratitude..."

Amazing progress is made when one learns to place themselves in a grateful state. Gratitude creates beautiful vibrations, and beautiful vibrations attract beautiful things to adorn the Path, things you will come in contact with on your journey. Your gratitude creates a more beautiful Path for you to travel upon.

Reflections:

_____

_____

_____

_____

_____

_____

_____

"Your fear of failure keeps you from putting forth your best effort..."

That fear is a product of your attachment to the outcome of that which you wish to accomplish. If you can learn to simply put forth your best effort while removing your attachment to the outcome, then the fear associated with failure would disappear as well.

Reflections:

_____

_____

_____

_____

_____

_____

_____

"The problem isn't with the resources you have available to use, the problem is with your level of belief/conviction..."

We have access to every resource in existence, but we won't attempt to make use of those resources until we accept the truth of that statement.

Reflections:

_____

_____

_____

_____

_____

_____

_____

_____

_____

"If you believe yourself to be incapable of accomplishing something, then it will be almost impossible for you to accomplish it..."

This isn't so much a spiritual concept, it is true because of the simple fact that most people won't attempt to do something they truly believe themselves to be incapable of doing. If you want to speed up the process of Ascension, begin to remove doubt from your mind. Allow yourself to believe without reservation.

Reflections:

_____

_____

_____

_____

_____

"The human concept of time as a linear construct is an illusion...."

And it is one that lays the foundation for and perpetuates many of the other illusions we fall victim to during our human experience. The idea of growing old, the idea of becoming weaker and more susceptible to illnesses because of it, and even the idea of a lack of progress are all products of a false idea of the nature of time.

Reflections:

"This world isn't an illusion, not according to the human idea of what an illusion is. The tree is as real as you or I Am, the illusion is the false idea of its purpose and the nature of its existence. The illusion has less to do with the tree's physical properties and more to do with our perspective, how we view the tree."

Reflections:

_____

_____

_____

_____

_____

_____

_____

_____

"They will hear when they are meant to, they will see when they are meant to, they will feel when they are meant to, according to Divine timing. Focus on your efforts, let go of the outcomes."

Reflections:

_____

_____

_____

_____

_____

_____

_____

_____

_____

About the Author

Joaquin Evans is a student of the Self Realization Fellowship and was heavily inspired by the life and works of Paramahansa Yogananda. More than that he is a student of life whose aspiration is to help others learn to reach new levels of happiness in their own lives. You can connect with him through social media on Instagram at @Joa301 or @MessagesToSelf #MessagesToSelf and on Facebook: https://www.facebook.com/Messages2Self

Acknowledgements

To my wife, who saw me before I learned to see myself. Thank you for sticking by me while I worked to find myself

To Q, thank you for coming on this wild ride with us and thank you for loving us so perfectly

To Geneva and Adam, thank you for believing and thank you for supporting the vision

To Stephanie Fahie, Kierra Jones, Laquita Anderson, Cherelle Kantey, Ethlynne Thomas, Matthew Beyer, Toye Dixon, Jycelis Torres, Bashea Williams, Llacey Simmons, CM Lugo, Christyn Day, Quotel Scott, Rafael Zubizaretta, Jesse Bryant, Sabrina Percario, Tiffany Payne,

Adele Williams, Adrian Noll, Ivory Perkins, Markel Coley, Jamie Henderson, Syreeta Clark & Roy Maxwell. Thank you for helping to bring this book to life.

And last but not least, thank you to every single person who said a prayer, spoke a kind word or sent some positive energy. I love you all, and I pray peace and blessings and deep-seated wisdom to you and yours

Made in the USA
Las Vegas, NV
16 July 2021